DODD, MEAD WONDER BOOKS

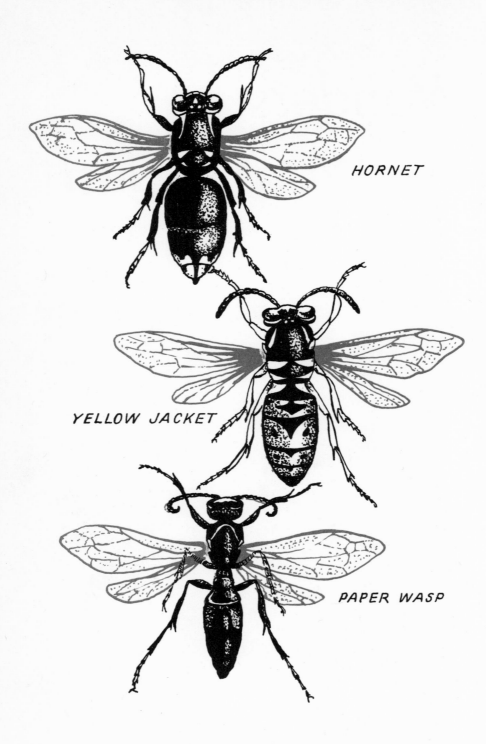

HORNET

YELLOW JACKET

PAPER WASP

Wonders of
the Wasp's Nest

BY SIGMUND A. LAVINE

Illustrated by Ernest H. Hart

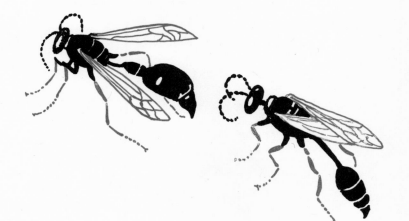

DODD, MEAD & COMPANY

New York

For Rose and Mark

Fellow Students of Nature

Contents

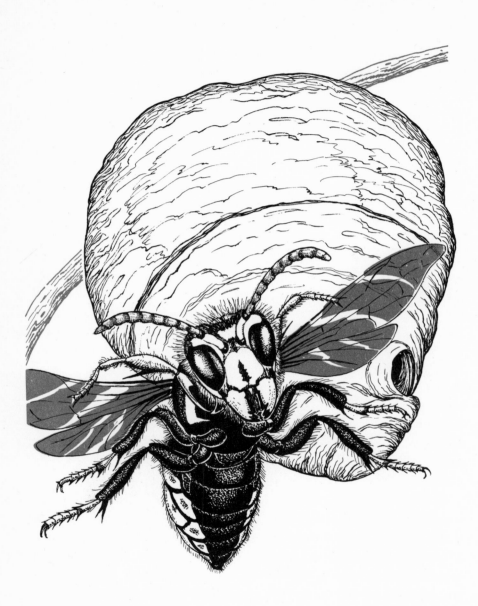

1. "A Bold and Troublesome Insect"

Man has an ancient prejudice against wasps—those slim-waisted insects with the long trailing legs so common to a sunny summer's day. He has been particularly unfair to the familiar stubby hornet and the colorful yellow jacket. Wasps, hornets and yellow jackets—these being common names for various members of the same insect family—will be referred to as wasps throughout this book, except where indicated, since it is their universal name. Although these maligned creatures do not deserve their reputation, until comparatively recent times most nature writers stressed the bad tempers and the "wickedness" of all wasps and gave the impression that they did nothing but sting people. Unfortunately, there are many who still believe this, despite the fact that we have learned that wasps never harm humans or animals unless molested. Yet, because they *will* sting whenever they decide an intruder means harm to them or their nests, wasps have not been the subject of as much study as those insects which attract attention because of their beauty, such as butterflies, or the species which supply mankind with valuable products, such as the silkworm.

However, entomologists (the technical word for students of insects) are slowly gathering information about wasps. Their scientific research shows that the "wicked wasp" is possibly the most intelligent of insects, engaging in amazing activities. There are, for example, wasp architects, air-conditioning experts, bricklayers, carpenters, health officers, hunters, masons, miners, nursemaids, papermakers, potters, parasites and policemen.

While investigating the ways of wasps, naturalists have discovered that they do far more good than harm. Of the more than 2500 species in North America, only about 50 are troublesome to man, damaging ripe fruit or destroying vegetation. The rest are among our best insect friends. Like bees, they carry pollen, the golden dust that makes possible all fruit and seeds, from one blossom to another, although they are not as active pollinators as the honey makers. Wasps are, however, a most important control of pests that prey on crops. Each year they kill millions of aphids, beetles, caterpillars, fruit flies and grasshoppers. This is why the United States Department of Agriculture has imported wasps from Africa to fight the pink bollworm in the South and others from the Orient to combat the gypsy moth in the Northeast.

Despite these facts, many people throughout the world still regard wasps as evil creatures. This is because our ancestors looked upon them as symbols of everything annoying and disagreeable. As a result, many superstitions about wasps are still believed, as well as ancient tales describing supernatural powers that supposedly enabled them to harm humans.

Strangely enough, however, man has long used wasps in medicine. Often a "prescription" containing wasps is far more painful than the ache it is supposed to soothe. The Kwakiutl Indians of the northwest coast mix nettles and a wasp nest into a ball and hold this mixture to their foreheads with a pair of tongs whenever they have a headache. Almost immediately the throbbing disappears—and there is good reason. The sting of the nettles and the angry wasps is so agonizing that the Indians can't feel the headache!

Wasp poultices are also used to relieve the pangs of rheumatism in rural sections of the American Middle West and as a cure for boils in the bluegrass region of Kentucky. On the other side of the world, in the Orient, this remedy is applied to horses suffering from colic or to those that have been bitten by snakes in hope of counteracting the venom.

Besides being used in folk medicine, wasps are important in folklore.

According to legend, the wasp is always wise, cunning and an associate of evildoers. Even cultured Romans thought them a sign of disaster. In 190 B.C., we are told, "an infinite number of wasps flew into the market at Capua, and sat in the temple of Mars. They were with great diligence taken and burnt solemnly. Yet they did foreshadow the coming of the enemy and the burning of the city."

It was commonly believed throughout Europe in medieval times that a wasp left a witch's body while she slept and flew about casting spells. Moreover, it was maintained that the witch could not be awakened until the wasp returned. Similarly, Siberian tribesmen were convinced that the soul of their shaman or medicine man, who alone could control the unseen world of demons and spirits, often took the shape of a wasp.

Because of their undeserved reputation for fierceness, wasps are prominent in tribal rites. Before the coming of civilization, Indians living on Vancouver Island rubbed the ashes of burned wasps into their faces before venturing into battle, assured that this ceremony would make them brave warriors. Today, deep in the jungle of French Guiana, natives force their children to submit to wasp stings so that they will learn to endure suffering. Evidently, they never heard of the ancient superstition of the Near East that 27 wasp stings will kill a man!

Wasps have been mentioned in literature since earliest times. There are several references to them in the Bible. Both ancient Latin and Greek authors allude to them, usually in an uncomplimentary manner. However, blind Homer pays wasps a pretty compliment in *The Illiad*. He calls them "beautiful and restless." Nor does the poet agree with those who thought wasps pugnacious, for, when the Greeks refuse to leave their ships and fight during the Trojan War, he has an angry warrior compare them to wasps guarding their nest. Both Aristophanes and Euripides, the famous Greek dramatists, deal with wasps in their plays. The former, who considered them the most peevish and irascible of creatures, used them as the basis of his satire, *The Wasps*. This play pokes fun at those who create quarrels with the idea of reaping a profit

9

from them. Euripides, when describing the plan of Ulysses and his men to poke out the single eye of Cyclops with a firebrand, compares their scheme to the way Athenian boys destroy wasps' nests.

Aristotle, the famous philosopher, was one of the few ancients who sought factual material about wasps. His *History of Animals,* published in 330 B.C., contains observations that modern investigators have confirmed. Yet his discoveries were forgotten during the Middle Ages, when wasps were the subjects of fear, and legend was often preferred to truth.

By the end of the sixteenth century, a few men, overcoming the traditional fear of wasps, were investigating their habits. However, they became hopelessly confused, frequently classifying them as bees. Meanwhile, the storytellers continued to spin yarns about the sly ways of the wasp.

When the early settlers came to America, they brought many Old World superstitions about wasps with them. Pioneers were convinced that wasps were weather prophets, and, in New England, children chanted:

> If hornets build low,
>   Winter storms and snow;
> If hornets build high,
>   Winter mild and dry.

This superstition probably had its origin in the belief that hornets remain in their nests during the winter, which they do not. However, many people still insist that the height at which wasps make their nests above water is an indication of the amount of rain that will fall during the summer. In a wet season, wasps are supposed to choose the top of a brook bank; in a dry one, almost the water's level. The truth is, various species build at different heights near water.

Although few people still hold that great numbers of hornets flying late in autumn mean storms at sea, many consider wasps an accurate means of foretelling weather. If they seem to bite more eagerly than

usual, it is a sign of rain! Superstition also states that if wasps fly about in groups before dusk, it is a sign that the next day will be hot and fair, but, if they seek shelter before twilight, it will storm.

Many beliefs dealing with wasps are contradictory. One is that the first wasp seen in the season should be killed, to insure good luck during the coming year. On the other hand, there is a conviction among some people that the first wasp should *not* be killed in order to avoid bad luck. In fact, some people consider it unlucky to ever kill a wasp. Others will tell you that, if wasps nest inside your house, it is a sure sign you are going to lose all your money!

One of the most charming stories told by the Indians of the Great Plains recounts how their ancestors learned the art of pottery and basket making from wasps.

Another famous piece of American folklore is a tall tale. However, you'll find just as many who claim it is true as those who call it a legend. At any rate, it is one of the few stories in which wasps are heroes. It relates how, during the War of 1812, a British man-of-war sailed up the Patuxent River in Maryland. The anchor was let go and a landing party, led by an officer in full dress, came ashore. The men wandered through a nearby village and met a small boy looking at a huge hornets' nest. The unwelcome visitors demanded to know what he was doing, and the youngster replied that he was about to cut down the nest of a rare hummingbird and catch it in a bag.

"What's so rare about it?" demanded the English officer.

"Well," replied the boy, "this bird cannot fly over water. But, if you want it, you can have it. Here, take this bag, cut the nest down with your sword and, when you are out to sea, open it up and you'll have a pet. I know the bird is in there, 'cause I can hear him."

The offer was accepted and the bag containing the nest was taken aboard. As soon as the vessel sailed out of the river into Chesapeake Bay, the bag was cut open, and the residents of the village, alerted by the quick-witted lad, peered through spyglasses and saw the officer and several of the crew jump overboard—but the villagers were sure they were not looking for a hummingbird!

Until this story is proven true, hornets are not entitled to a place in American history. However, hornets and wasps have long been a part of our idiomatic speech. Ill-tempered persons are often called "wasp-ish" or "waspy," an angry individual accused of being "mad as a hornet," while a troublemaker is said to be "stirring up a hornet's nest." All of which proves that most people know only one thing about wasps and hornets—that these insects become outraged when someone destroys their nests. But after all, wouldn't you?

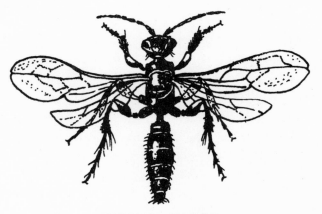

TIPHID WASP

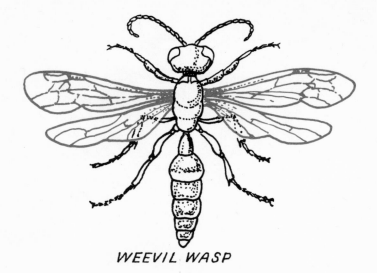

WEEVIL WASP

2. What Is a Wasp?

Wasps are members of the largest group of animals in the world, the insects. Found everywhere except in the depths of the ocean, insects have successfully lived on this earth for 200 million years. Their ancestor was probably a wormlike creature; yet most of the 12,000 identified fossil insects resemble those of the present day.

The word "insect" comes from the Latin "in sections" and is most appropriate, for the body is divided into three segments: the head, thorax or middle part, and the abdomen. Their scientific name, Hexapoda, derived from the Greek *hex* (six) and *poda* (feet), is also descriptive, as all true insects walk on six legs.

Entomologists claim that the average back yard is the home of at least a thousand different species of insects and conservatively estimate

that more than two million species exist. They have already identified over half a million. In order to study insects' life histories, naturalists classify them in "orders"—groups having the same characteristics. Wasps and their close relatives, ants and bees, belong to the order Hymenoptera, a word made from the Greek *hymen* (membrane) and *pteron* (wing). There are 100,000 known species of Hymenoptera.

Although about 17,000 species of wasps have been identified and scientists are constantly classifying new ones, it is not easy to recognize a wasp. For there are bees that look like wasps, wasps that look like bees, and wasps that look like ants. To add confusion, some defenseless flies mimic the coloring of certain wasps in order to frighten away their enemies.

However, while hornets and yellow jackets have comparatively stout, rather short bodies, generally speaking, wasps are slender-bodied insects, have four wings and a characteristic narrow "waist." Their commonest colors are black, smoky-gray, brown, yellow, orange and red. Many of them, like the sometimes too familiar yellow jackets and hornets, are marked with crosswise bands or rings.

Wasps are separated into two groupings by entomologists: true wasps and all other wasps. To a naturalist, true wasps are those which, unlike most Hymenoptera, have the habit of folding their wings fanlike down the middle. Other wasps do not pleat their wings but keep them flat on their backs when at rest. For further convenience, wasps are divided into two additional groups depending on whether they live alone, as do most insects, or in communities, as do the hornets, yellow jackets and other papermakers. Wasps that live alone are commonly called solitary wasps; those that form colonies, social wasps. To entomologists they are known as Sphecoidea and Vespoidea respectively.

SPHECOIDEA

The vast majority of known species of wasps are solitary in habit. Each female makes a nest—or several—in the location favored by her species. Some excavate burrows in the ground, others mold clay into various shapes, still others bore tunnels in trees, posts or pithy stems. When the nest is completed, the female goes hunting for the particular species of food that her ancestors have sought for centuries. After paralyzing her prey by stinging, she carries it to the nest, repeating the process until she has stored enough food to supply her babies until they are old enough to care for themselves.

Because many solitary wasps nest in the ground they are commonly called digger wasps and known scientifically as fossores, from the Latin *fossor* (a digger). Though they do not live in colonies, some diggers seem to enjoy the companionship of others of the same species, and a number of females often excavate their burrows near one another.

As indicated, all solitary wasps are hunters. Each species preys on a certain spider or insect and may confine itself to capturing only the males or females among the game it seeks. There is just as much specialization in the "blueprints" they follow in their nest-building and food-stocking methods. They also vary in size and appearance. Some are extremely small, others quite large. While various species dress demurely in drab black, others flaunt coats of brilliant metallic blues and reds.

Sphecoidea are among the most interesting of insects. Despite their definite habit patterns, individual wasps show extraordinary ability to adapt to changing conditions.

VESPOIDEA

There are about 800 species of Vespoidea. Most of them manufacture paper from wood fibers to build their nests. In the temperate zone, their colonies are started by an overwintering queen. When spring comes, she builds a few cells of the comb, laying an egg in each. When the young wasps hatch they take over the task of enlarging the nest. Their skillful architecture is fully described in the chapter dealing with wasp papermakers.

Because scientists have classified all true wasps as Vespoidea, not all the species included under this heading are social in habit. Those that are solitary burrow in the ground or make tiny clay urns to hold their eggs. Incidentally, social wasps were once solitary in habit. Over the centuries, like man, they have learned the value of living together for protection, as well as the fact that it is easier to do a task if a group co-operates.

Some social wasps form small colonies and build crude nests; others gather in communities of thousands and live in elaborate, long-lasting apartments. You can tell which species occupies a nest by its shape and location. The large pear-shaped nests of the white-faced hornet are always suspended from trees and shrubs. Those of the giant hornet, introduced into this country from Europe in 1852, are placed in hollow trees, stumps or under a porch or roof. They are globular in shape. Yellow jackets—there are half a dozen species in the United States, all looking very much alike—place their paper cities underground.

You probably have seen both *Polistes* (a social wasp that has no common name) and its nest, for these rather large wasps, about one inch long, reddish-black or brown with smoky wings, are common throughout the United States. Their nests, which consist of an un-protected flat comb hanging from a short central stem, are placed in a corner of a building, under eaves, around windows, behind blinds or against a door frame.

Found all over the world, Vespoidea vary in color and size as do the humans in whose countries they thrive, and like humans, they have a wide range of habits.

The details of any wasp's body—social or solitary—are best seen under the lens of a microscope or a magnifying glass. So let's examine a specimen under magnification.

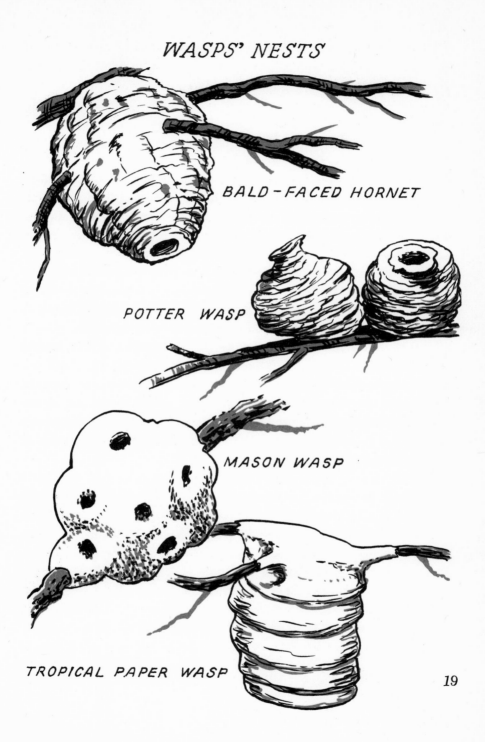

WASPS' NESTS

BALD-FACED HORNET

POTTER WASP

MASON WASP

TROPICAL PAPER WASP

19

3. Under the Lens

Our first discovery is that, while wasps appear to be bald, they are, like all Hymenoptera, actually covered with a thick coat of hair. However, their "fur coat," unlike that of bees, is never branched nor barbed, feathery, or pointed like that of ants.

A lens also shows the details of the strong but flexible covering which serves insects that have no bones as a skeleton. Composed of many thick plates, this armor, called exoskeleton by scientists, protects the internal organs and provides an attachment for the muscles which connect to its inside surface. This coat of mail is so rigid that, were it not for elastic connections between the plates, insects would be unable to move.

The three ringlike segments that make up the body—the head, thorax and abdomen—are clearly seen under magnification. Each segment has definite functions. The head contains the eyes, antennae, brain and mouth; the thorax supports the wings and legs; the abdomen, the vital organs and, in female wasps, the sting.

EYES

Wasps have two sets of eyes—a pair of large compound eyes consisting of many tiny eyes massed together on either side of their variously shaped heads, and a pair of simple eyes that form a triangle on the top of the forehead. Simple eyes are sensitive to light, but cannot form an image. On the other hand, each of the hundreds of hexagonal facets that make up the compound eye sends to the brain (which, considering a wasp's size, is very big) an impression of a small section of the object at which the insect is looking. Here, each part is joined together with the others to form a complete picture, just as a jig-saw puzzle is put together.

Although compound eyes don't give as clear a picture as ours do, wasps have excellent eyesight, the males having larger eyes than females. To a wasp, objects at some distance are equivalent to relatively smaller objects nearby. Unlike humans, wasps cannot focus or close their eyes, but can distinguish ultraviolet light, totally invisible to us. The ability of wasps to recognize colors was discovered by the world-renowned, husband-and-wife team of entomologists, George and Elizabeth Peckham of Milwaukee, who placed different-colored paper with openings for the insects to go through over the entrance holes of ground wasps.

They found that wasps located their nests faster when they were covered with blue paper than with red, and that, once the insects had become familiar with a blue doorway, they had great difficulty in finding their homes if the blue cover was removed. After leaving a

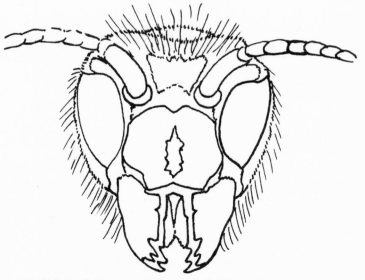

HEAD OF WHITE-FACED HORNET

blue paper over the entrances for a week, the Peckhams exchanged it for a yellow one, placing the blue sheet a short distance away. The wasps flew immediately to the blue covering, milling about or trying to dig beneath it, hoping to find the nest. Eventually, one located the entrance hole in the yellow paper and led the others home. Experiments proved that wasps found their nests faster when covered with a shade new to them than when they were uncovered—showing that the insects were guided by color.

MOUTH

Designed for biting and chewing, a wasp's mouth consists of a front lip; sidewise moving jaws called mandibles; a pair of complicated organs known as maxillae, used to pick up, hold and taste food; and a second pair of maxillae that form the lower lip. The mandibles of wasps, which contain teeth for cutting, sawing and tearing, vary greatly

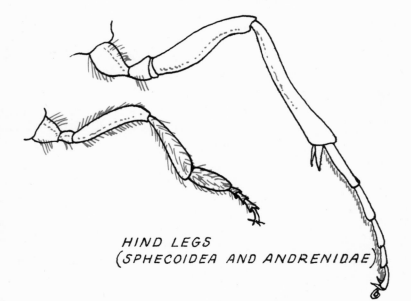

HIND LEGS
(SPHECOIDEA AND ANDRENIDAE)

in shape—in some species they resemble a bird's beak!

Like bees, adult wasps feed on nectar, but they secure it only from shallow flowers. This is because their sucking tubes, formed by a fusing of certain mouth parts, are far shorter and less efficient than those of their cousins. However, their powerful jaws allow them to chew their prey and then they have no trouble lapping up the exuding juices.

ANTENNAE

Wasps have no noses, but they can smell; they have no fingers, but they can feel; and, though unable to speak, they talk to one another!

All these activities are performed with their antennae, the pair of feelers set between the eyes. Antennae serve wasps as organs of taste, touch and smell—and, some naturalists think, of hearing. They are attached to the head by a ball-and-socket joint, which enables them to be turned in all directions like "rabbit ear" aerials on TV sets. Wasps' antennae vary greatly in appearance. Some are elbowed in the middle, others are club shaped, slender, stout or threadlike. Often there is a difference in the antennae of males and females of the same species, but, no matter what their form, antennae consist of two parts: a stiff stocky handle and a flexible tip composed of small joints covered with minute sense organs.

Wasps have a keen sense of smell. Their antennae are so sensitive to air-borne odors that they can pick up the scent of food from a considerable distance—particularly that of animal origin. In one experiment, they readily found a cloth hidden in deep grass that had been scented with meat but paid no attention to dishes filled with peppermint, wintergreen and cloves. Before eating anything, wasps test its edibility by running their antennae over it—just as we place the tip of our tongues in a spoonful of medicine to see if it is bitter or sweet.

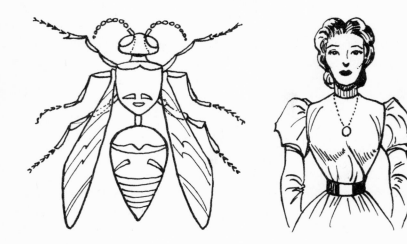

When wasps touch food with their feelers, they are really "tasting" it, for they sense flavor by touch.

The sense of touch is far more developed in wasps than in humans. While humans rely upon their eyes to recognize friends, wasps pat each other with their feelers. If from the same nest, they carry on a "conversation" by stroking each other. Unlike bees, which are apt to fight with strangers, wasps merely back away, waving their antennae in final salute. Moreover, wasps do not communicate with one another, as bees do, to tell of a source of food—perhaps because they rarely find a large store of food in one place.

THORAX

The thorax, or middle division of the body, is divided into three segments which support the legs and wings and surround the muscles that move them. Solitary wasps have a square thorax which limits the movements of their heads—compensated for by having larger eyes than the social species whose rounded thorax permits free movement. At the end of the third segment, in many species, there is a very slender joint called the petiole that connects the thorax to the abdomen. This characteristic is the source of the term "wasp-waisted," which is applied to women with small waists. It was first used by Aristophanes, who ridiculed Greek ladies of fashion for trying to look like wasps.

LEGS

Each segment of the thorax bears a pair of jointed legs made up of five sections that fit together like a curtain rod and end in a clawlike foot. Hair-covered pads on the feet enable wasps to walk over smooth surfaces, but they move more quickly across rough material where they can use their claws. The claws of solitary wasps only are equipped with teeth which they use when digging, making cement or boring in wood. All wasps, however, can "taste" with their feet and can tell

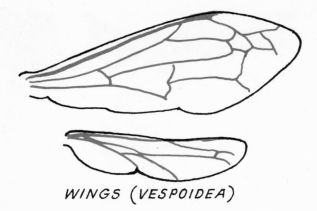

WINGS (VESPOIDEA)

whether water has been salted or sugared by walking through it.

Walking or running wasps move their legs in alternate groups of three, the weight of the body always being upheld by a tripod—the best mechanical means of support. Some species have very long front legs, others long hind ones, but all are designed to allow the insects to excavate soil or carry heavy loads. Wasps' legs have to be sturdy, for these insects can pull 20 times their own weight—man pulls slightly less than nine-tenths of his!

Wasps also use their legs as whisk brooms. Whenever their antennae are dusty, they slide them between a tiny prong and a curved groove on the forelegs. As a feeler moves along, the prong's edges and the groove's teeth remove all dust. Wasps clean their faces just as cats do, using their "paws" as facecloths. The feet themselves are scrubbed by being drawn over the abdomen.

WINGS

Very few wasps are wingless. Most have two sets of wings. They are of cellophane-like texture, the hind pair being considerably smaller and fastening to the rear edges of the front pair by tiny hooks, so that

only one surface is presented to the air. Wasps are strong flyers, capable of a speed of 30 miles an hour, beating their wings 110 times a second in a figure-of-eight—up, forward, down and back—a fact discovered by Sir John Lubbock who, late in the nineteenth century, pasted gold leaf on the wings of wasps so that he could watch them in flight.

The familiar buzz made by wasps is caused by the vibration of their wings. The faster they move, the more noise. It has been determined that the sound made by the wings of an angry yellow jacket is equal to A in the second octave below middle C; that of an annoyed *Vespa*, G# in the same octave—but few musicians are curious enough to confirm this with a tuning fork when about to be stung!

ABDOMEN

Wasps' abdomens vary greatly in size and shape and may be longer or shorter than the rest of the body. Tiny holes along the sides of the segments admit air to a complicated system of small tubes that supply oxygen to all parts of the body, wasps, like all insects, having neither nostrils nor lungs. Many of these tubes are thinner than a human hair but are lined with a spirally coiled thread of cuticle-like material which keeps them open. The thin, watery, yellowish-green blood of insects plays no part in their respiration; therefore each abdominal segment is independent of the others for oxygen. Thus, insects are capable of withstanding mutilations that would kill animals that rely on blood to carry oxygen through their bodies.

The abdomen also contains digestive organs. Food passes from the mouth through a narrow gullet and the crop to the thorax, where digestion begins. In the crop, food is temporarily stored, an arrangement which makes it possible for a wasp to regurgitate and share his meal with other wasps. Wasp-waisted species never have a "solid" meal—only liquids can reach their abdomens—for the food passageway shares space in the petiole with an artery, nerve cords, muscles and breathing tubes.

STING

At the tip of a female's abdomen is the egg-laying apparatus or ovipositor. In wasps, as in bees and many ants, this mechanism has been modified to act as a poison-injecting sting, the eggs passing out of an opening at its base and not through the ovipositor itself. Only female Hymenoptera have stings; all other insects use their mouths to inflict wounds. Solitaries use stings to paralyze or kill their prey, socials employ theirs solely as a means of defense.

Far sharper than a man-made needle, a wasp's sting easily penetrates the skin of a victim and injects a venom so powerful that a microscopic drop can paralyze 1,600 caterpillars! Each species has its own poison formula, and the stings of solitary and social wasps are slightly different in construction. The former are barbless; the latter, barbed like those of bees. However, social wasps can readily withdraw their stings and use them many times. Bees usually die after stinging, being too excited to take time to release the barbs by a movement similar to that used to take a corkscrew out of a cork. Moreover, while bees rush at an enemy and sting anywhere, wasps take their time and look for a favorable spot; thus they rarely catch their stings on clothing.

When a social wasp stings, the pointed ovipositor is thrust into the victim like a dagger and plunged deep into tissue beneath the skin. Then two barbed, serrated needles driven by powerful muscles shoot out and alternately strike with a rapid movement that carries them deeper into the wound. Meanwhile, venom is pumped from the poison sac in the abdomen and emerges from the ends of the needles and the sides of the six barbs. Finally, the wasp pulls the barbs upward, opening the flesh so that the venom can spread.

Solitary wasps are like skilled swordsmen; they drive their barbless rapier into a nerve center despite all attempts to parry. Some of these winged killers produce poison so powerful that *one* part of it in 200,000,000 parts of blood can paralyze an insect. However, humans need never fear the sting of any wasps if they remember a simple rule—let them alone and never disturb their nests!

4. The Wasp Family

A colony of social wasps gathered for a family dinner would require a tremendous table. As many as 25,000 individuals may live together in a single nest.

From spring until fall, a community of social wasps consists of an egg-laying female misnamed the queen, for she does not rule but is merely the foundress of the family, and a great number of her daughters known as workers. When nights grow cool, the queen lays eggs that hatch males called drones. Every resident of the nest has definite tasks, all work for the others and never think of themselves. While each "caste" resembles the others in appearance, as do the members of all families, the various classes have certain physical characteristics that enable them to carry out their duties.

THE WILLING WORKER

With the exception of laying eggs that hatch wasps of all castes, workers perform all necessary chores to keep the community alive. Actually undeveloped females, workers even try to save the colony when the queen dies by laying eggs, but only males develop from them.

Workers labor from dawn to dusk, obeying no time clock but the sun. During the first three weeks of life, a worker hunts for food and for materials to repair and enlarge the nest. Then, no longer able to make paper—having exhausted her supply of the fluid that glues wood fibers together while being chewed—she becomes a nursemaid and housekeeper. A few weeks later, completely worn out, she dies.

While adult social wasps feed mostly upon nectar, fruit juices and fermenting sap, insects and spiders form the diet of their babies. To supply them, small prey is killed in flight; larger game stung to death, then chewed. The juices are swallowed and stored in the crop, while the finely ground flesh is formed into a ball and carried home between the mandibles.

Arriving at the nest, a forager is surrounded by housekeepers who beg for food. She bends sidewise and regurgitates a drop of liquid, which sticks to her broad tongue from which her sisters lick it. Most of the liquid received by house wasps is passed on to others in the same way, one drop serving to supply dozens of stay-at-homes. When

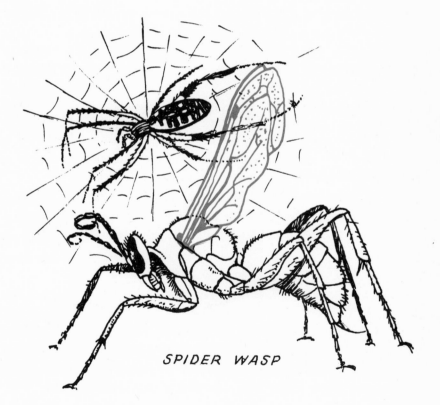

SPIDER WASP

a forager's crop is emptied, she goes looking for more food.

Nurse wasps feed the youngest babies a secretion manufactured in their bodies and older ones with insect patties, rolling the pellets with their front legs just as a human pats hamburger into shape. The babies lift their heads at mealtime, open their jaws and emit a drop of sweet saliva that moistens the food so that it slides down easily. If there is no saliva, workers gently seize the heads of their charges in their mandibles and pull them back and forth in their nurseries to stimulate its flow. Because all wasps enjoy drinking this liquid, babies are often "milked" without being fed. Therefore wasps take more from them than they give—young workers taking the most—but their desire for the sweet makes for a close association between adults and young, a fundamental of social organization among insects. Scientists call this reciprocal feeding "trophallaxis."

A group of workers who act as ladies-in-waiting supply food to the queen. Others clean the nest. If an individual wasp cannot remove an object—they never co-operate in such tasks as ants do—it is covered over with thick paper. Still others guard the nest's entrance or ventilate the interior by fanning their wings vigorously. If the nest becomes flooded, house wasps suck up the water, fly outside and dispose of it. On extremely hot days, workers fill their crops with water and regurgitate over the sides of the nest to make it cooler.

Some workers are quite small—particularly those born in the early days of the colony—but all have the strength and ability to do their various tasks and help protect their home from harm.

THE LAZY DRONE

Male wasps lead happy lives. They spend their days flitting from flower to flower, sipping nectar or resting in the sun. If the weather is overcast, drones crawl headfirst into an empty cell and take a nap.

Usually drones are bigger than workers, although some are not so well developed as others and, in a few species, are scarcely larger than their sisters. They have long drooping antennae and strong wings that enable them to buzz ferociously, but drones are harmless, having no sting. Males exist for just one purpose, to mate with a young queen.

Just before cold weather, drones and queens leave the nests and fly high in the sky. Far above the earth they sail off in a marriage flight, but soon separate. The males die shortly thereafter, or are killed by their wives, but the fertilized females seek a sheltered spot and hibernate all winter.

HER MAJESTY, THE QUEEN

Born in a cell larger than those that cradle commoners, social wasps of royal blood receive special attention from workers, who supply them constantly with food. As a result, queens are the largest wasps in a nest.

Awakening from her winter sleep, a queen seeks a suitable nesting

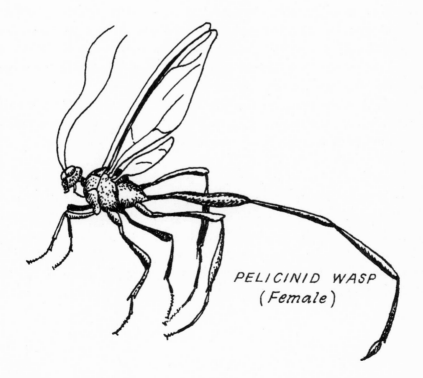

PELICINID WASP
(Female)

site. After locating one, Her Royal Highness manufactures paper and constructs a small cup containing a few shallow cells and places an egg in each. Because the cells open downward, she glues every egg in place with an oily substance made in her body. The sides of the cells are then raised and the nest enlarged, but the queen leaves the task of expanding it into its final form to her soon-to-be-born daughters. Nor does she lay any more eggs until those in the original cells hatch.

All of the first brood are workers, and their mother feeds them on "insectburgers." By the time they are full grown, another batch of eggs has hatched, but the queen pays no attention to this generation. The chore of caring for their younger sisters is taken over by the matured workers. Now Her Majesty does nothing but lay eggs, depositing as many as 25,000 in a season. She does not leave the nest until her reign comes to an end. For, with the first frost, all activity stops: no food is brought to the nest, no repairs are made. Workers drag the half-grown brood out of the cells to die and then die themselves, as does the enfeebled queen. Unmated drones are the last to perish and may often be seen on late-blooming flowers in Indian summer. Only the young, fertilized queens hibernate and survive the winter.

However, in the tropics—the original home of all wasps—some social species live in permanent colonies. They swarm like hive bees when the community grows too large for the available food supply but store no honey in their nests. Other tropical wasps have a strange relationship with their first brood, all true females. These young queens stay with their mother for several weeks helping her before leaving to establish colonies of their own.

Polistes, unlike most social insects, frequently have more than one queen in their communities. In eastern North America, a queen may found a colony alone or be joined by several others. Quite often the original queen dissolves this partnership and joins another. Yet everywhere else in the temperate zone—*Polistes* having almost world-wide distribution—this species, like honeybees, does not tolerate more than one queen in a nest.

34

There are no workers among solitary wasps, only males and females. The latter build the nest, provision it and care for their young without ever having seen another wasp perform any of these chores. Most solitaries, after stocking their nests, lay their eggs, seal them up and never return. This is called mass provisioning. The brood develops and leaves its combination nursery and dining room without help. A few solitaries, however, care for their young, bringing them food just as a mother bird attends to fledglings. This is known as progressive provisioning. It is the first step wasps make toward becoming a social species.

Most solitary males die after mating. One exception is Mr. *Trypoxylon rubrocinctus,* who helps his wife set up house in an abandoned tunnel once used by wood-boring beetles as a home. He stands guard in the entrance hole while the female is out hunting. When she returns, he scrambles out and she carries him pickaback into their nest!

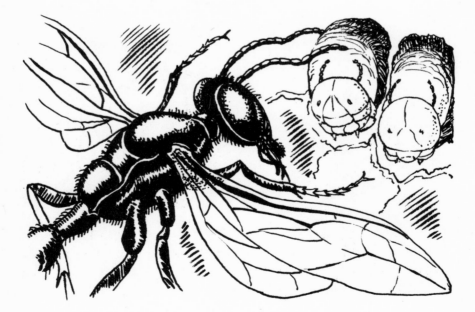

5. Wasp Babies

Wasp babies do not resemble their parents until they reach their adult or "imaginal" form. Like all Hymenoptera, wasps develop in four stages—egg, larva, pupa, adult—a process known as metamorphosis. This Greek word means "to change shape."

EGG

While solitary females may lay as few as six eggs, social queens deposit anywhere from a few hundred to many thousands in the cells built by their daughters. The eggs of social wasps are long, white and slightly curved, but those of solitaries vary in appearance. They may be cylindrical, oval or look like miniature walrus tusks. No matter what their shape, all hatch out in two or three days, whether in nurseries made of paper, earth, hollow stems, grass or cement-like mud.

LARVA

The soft whitish, maggot-like grub that emerges from the egg is called a larva (plural, larvae). A larva lacks compound eyes, wings and legs, although its body is segmented. Moreover, its mouth parts are well developed and, like all babies, wasp larvae are happiest when eating.

Among the solitaries that practice mass provisioning, feeding larvae is no problem. The grubs dine upon the paralyzed insects on which the eggs had been laid, and the supply of fresh meat lasts until they are capable of caring for themselves. Solitaries that engage in progressive provisioning—they lay the fewest eggs—have a much harder task. *Bembix pruinosa,* for example, a sand wasp common in North America, feeds its larvae only soft parts of flies, and it takes twenty a day to satisfy each grub. Mother wasp lines the flies along the floor of the nest which she has dug two feet below the surface of the dunes, and the baby wiggles along eating in cafeteria style. When a larva is full grown and ready to pupate, the entrance to the nest is sealed, a new nursery dug and an egg placed inside. But *pruinosa* has little rest. In two days, another grub is demanding to be fed.

Because the cells of all social wasps face downward, their larvae are not as comfortable in their cradles as those of the hive bees who have horizontal nurseries. In fact, if the queen did not glue each egg to the cell walls, most social-wasp larvae would tumble out headfirst. As it is, they have to be acrobats to survive. When the grubs hatch, they keep their tailends in the eggshell and, by pivoting on them, are able to crane their heads to the cell opening to receive food from the workers. As they grow, they constantly change position with the help of their jaws and a sucker-like foot at their lower ends. However, if they do not hold on with one end before securing a grip at the other, they fall out of their cradles. It would seem that wise wasps would realize that vertical cells opening downward are not safe for babies, but they never do. Nor do they attempt to replace infants that have tumbled out of their cribs. Workers just carry them out to the dump that social wasps maintain some distance from their nests.

Within a few days, larvae get so fat that the sides of the cells fit snugly around their bodies, and they no longer have to keep the sucker foot tight against the nursery roof. They gain weight so quickly that, if they wore clothes, the seams would have to be let out continually, but their exoskeletons cannot expand. Unable to remodel their "suits," larvae grow larger ones beneath their armor, which splits, exposing the new covering that hardens in the air. This is called molting. But soon the skin is again too tight and the process is repeated, the number of molts depending upon the species.

38

Despite meals of meat, nectar and fruit juice, larvae often feel neglected and "bawl" by scraping the walls of their cells with their jaws. Incidentally, when nurse wasps rob their charges of saliva and deliberately underfeed them, the larvae mature as undeveloped females. Thus the community's supply of workers is increased.

The larval stage of social wasps lasts between twelve and eighteen days. When full grown, larvae encase themselves in a wrapping of silk that they spin out of their mouths. These coverings are known as cocoons. Some are clear as cellophane, others parchment like, while those of digger wasps contain bits of sand and other coarse materials. Solitary wasps' cocoons are fastened to the sides of the nest built by the female before laying her eggs; those of social wasps to the cell walls, the openings of which are then capped with silk. In either case, cocoons are a sign stating: ALTERATIONS GOING ON, PUPA AT WORK!

PUPA

Although all seems quiet under the silk, great changes are taking place. Slowly the body turns dark, its three divisions appear, and the eyes, legs and wings take shape. The pupal stage of social wasps lasts eighteen days and, when fully grown, the adults bite through the cap and crawl to the nearest larva to beg a drink. In a week, they are helping their older sisters. Similarly, mature solitaries gnaw their way through the adobe or wood that sheltered them, or dig their way to the surface. Many solitary wasps pupate all winter—an insurance that they will survive the cold.

6. Wasp Architecture

If wasps employed architects to design their nests, they would never consider any plan that called for an unusual arrangement of rooms. They prefer age-old patterns; fossil nests 80,000,000 years old look exactly the same as those of today.

Wasps make homes of various sizes and shapes out of a wide range of materials. Some make paper nests that look like delicate lace, others like sheets of heavy cardboard. Still others found in the East Indies make massive mud mansions, though most wasp masons mold small, fine nests. *Chlorion auripes* builds with grass, selecting each blade with great care. When *auripes* finds a satisfactory one, she walks along it as if measuring, saws off a length and, as it breaks off, flies away with her prize. At her nesting site, an abandoned bumblebee hole, she tucks her load into position. The blade fits perfectly, and, when the nest is finished, it resembles that of a bird.

Each species has its specialized methods of construction and places its nest in definite locations. As previously mentioned, some social species nest above ground, others below. Most solitaries burrow in the earth—some biting the soil out in chunks, others kicking it out with their legs, still others carrying it out in "armfuls." A few tunnel under bark or sublet the deserted galleries made by beetles in decaying wood, while some take advantage of any cavity. They may set up housekeeping in hollow twigs, keyholes, between the covers of books, or in a piece of unused pipe, rearing mud partitions to protect their eggs. One mud dauber found an ideal apartment between the half-closed hands of a religious statue in Poughkeepsie, New York.

Usually wasps are very consistent in their nesting habits. However, individuals, like human construction workers, vary greatly in skill. Some are careless; others are exceptionally particular and, if dissatisfied with their work, do it over again.

Some wasps' nests are no bigger than a quarter, others are tremendous. Generally the nests of tropical species are larger than those that live in cooler climates. In Ceylon, a papermaker builds a nest six feet long, while the home of a South American wasp, made of earth with paper walls as solid as stone, is equally large. Irrespective of their size, nests are able to withstand an amazing amount of moisture, many of them hanging exposed to rain without protection. However, in British Guiana, where hurricanes are frequent, wasps cover their homes with a specially made white, polished cardboard which keeps the inside perfectly dry.

While mason wasps mold nests of fantastic shapes and digger wasps are extremely clever builders—one desert species actually tops its burrow with a curved chimney made of pellets bitten out of the sun-baked ground—social wasps' nests in temperate climates show little variation. Those of hornets are either pear-shaped or look like a large grey balloon. Yellow jackets' underground nests also resemble a balloon, but are brown in color. The flat, circular homes of *Polistes*, suspended from a support by a stem, look rather like an oversized, inverted paper wineglass.

The most unusual nests are built by wasps living in the tropics. A social wasp found in South America constructs a baglike nest several feet long and encases it in a hard rindlike covering. Another species also makes enormous nests with the same type of covering, but ornaments them with dozens of projections. Unwary travelers often mistake this nest for a strange tropical fruit! Still another resident of South America builds its comb along the trunk of a tree, shielding it from the elements with thick paper.

Wasps' nests in the Old World tropics also show a great variety of form and size. Here, the insects nest between leaves pasted together with sticky material or make dwellings that look like upside-down mushrooms; short, frayed pieces of rope; peanuts strung together or sea shells. The home of one species is composed of half-a-dozen "ice cream cones" nestled together—but these wouldn't hold a large scoop of your favorite flavor, for the entire nest is scarcely three inches long. A wasp native to the Philippine Islands erects umbrella-like coverings above its nest to keep it dry—resembling the guards placed on ropes to prevent rats from leaving a ship that has visited a plague-infested port.

Each species of wasps furnishes its home in a certain way, whether it is a temporary structure built to last for a season in the temperate zone or a permanent dwelling in the tropics. While solitary wasps are content if their nests contain a pantry for food and a nursery for their

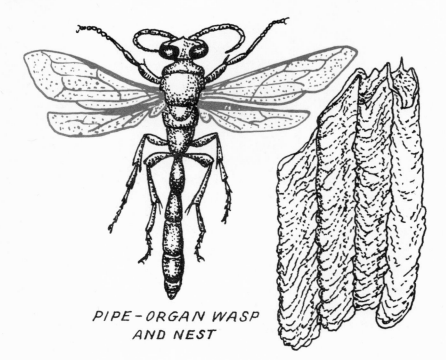

PIPE-ORGAN WASP
AND NEST

babies, social wasps are constantly making their houses more livable—
they add complicated passageways and bedrooms with built-in bunks,
erect ramps, and insulate the outside walls which they keep extending
by working from the inside.

7. Wonderful Wasps

While entomologists know that no insect can plan any action in advance, the cleverness and ingenuity of individual wasps make it appear that they realize what they are doing. While each species is controlled by definite instincts, certain wasps show an aptitude for learning and the ability to profit by experience. One mud dauber, trained by Professor George Shafer to eat honey from his hand while he stroked it, flew up to him three weeks after being released and landed on the exact finger always used to feed it!

Although their exoskeletons prevent facial expression, wasps express emotions. Hunters beat their wings furiously when they fail to sting their prey. Diggers quiver with delight when they find soil suitable for their burrows. Newly hatched *Bembix* males gather together in the warm spring sun and join in a joyful aerial dance while waiting for the females to emerge. When they do, the males return to the ground and engage in a mass struggle to win the affection of one of the ladies. Mated pairs, flying off on their honeymoons, are pursued by the rejected suitors.

The instincts of wasps vary greatly. The spider hunters, for example, show this in the way they carry prey. One species grabs the spider anywhere it can get a grip, drags it along the ground—even if it is so small it could be lifted—and walks backward; another wings along with its burden pressed tightly against the thorax by the second pair of legs. Often, instinctive actions such as these make more work. When carrying game, many hunters climb backward up plants in order to have a "launching pad" from which to soar down to their nests. Actually, unless the grass is tall and smooth, the struggle to the take-off point is not worthwhile. But this makes no difference to the wasps.

On the other hand, some wasps refuse to carry a heavy victim to a distant nest but build one close by instead. Yet many wasps tote loads for considerable distances. To expend as much effort, a man would have to carry a 200-pound pack for miles over rough ground. However, the long-legged and slender *Ammophila* that hunts caterpillars three or four times its own weight has devised a labor-saving technique. The caterpillars are a tremendous burden but are handled easily by these clever wasps, which turn the big worms over on their backs so that they slide smoothly along.

Naturalists have recorded watching wasps struggle up sheer cliffs through tangled underbrush with their prey. Nothing reported is more amazing than the account of a hunter who wearied of dragging a large caterpillar. The wasp raised the lower end and propped it against a blade of grass, swung the other end around to a slightly higher point, then alternately lifted each end just as a man would move a heavy load alone!

Among the spider hunters are those whose instinct is to leave their prey on the ground while they excavate their nests. Scientists have seen a number carefully hang the spider on a twig so that it will not be stolen by ants while they dig. Incidentally, though most wasps are honest, some are thieves and steal from their fellows.

During a drought, some diggers carry water to their nesting site to moisten the soil, so that they can pick it up in pellets. They belong to the species that burrow by biting, and it never occurs to them to kick the dry earth out with their legs. But they are "wise" enough to wet the soil.

These actions and others have convinced entomologists, who, like all naturalists, avoid endowing insects with human characteristics, that wasps have intelligence which they are using to find the most suitable way to live. While their relations, ants and bees, have been doing things in the same way for millions of years, wasps are still experimenting. It would take many books to detail all their amazing activities, but here are the stories of some truly wonderful wasps.

CARPENTERS

Carpentry is no longer a popular trade among wasps. Many species were once woodworkers, but are now apprentice masons. Instead of chiseling homes, they adapt an available opening to their purpose, separating each nursery cell with partitions of clay, earth or sawdust. Age-old instincts, however, incline them toward choosing galleries abandoned by wood-boring insects.

Usually these tunnels are enlarged by members of the *Odynerous* clan. They enter them headfirst, chew with their jaws and then either fly or walk backward to remove the sawdust. Most of these wasps practice mass provisioning and stock their nurseries with aphids, caterpillars, flies, grasshoppers, moths or spiders. Eggs hatch quickly, but the pupal state lasts all winter, cocoons frequently being mixed with the material used to make the partitions.

Some carpenters dig out stems or gnaw tunnels in weathered wood with their auger-like jaws. Others bite deep into twigs or bore into roots. But none works harder than *Crabo stripicola*, a tiny black wasp marked with yellow.

Stripicola bites pith out in pellets, passing these "shavings" back with her mandibles between her front legs until a pile accumulates. Then, walking backward up the stem, she pushes it out by kicking with her hind legs. This is a much more lengthy process than the one employed by *Crabo semaculatas*, a close relation, who nests in roots. These females only have to fan their wings just above the ground to blow away the sawdust. But *stripicola* never worries about overtime. Unlike most wasps, which work only during daylight, she never stops to rest until her job is done.

While all agree that ants and bees are willing workers, the record for industry belongs to one of the *stripicola*, who toiled for 42 hours with only a ten-minute "coffee break" before her ten-inch-long, three-and-one-half-inch-wide tunnel was completed. She spent the next three days catching enough flies to stock ten pith-partitioned cells and laying an egg in each. Her labors over, *stripicola* made full use of the extra chamber in her nest that she, like many of her species, build as bedrooms for themselves.

FRUITERERS

The fig was one of the first plants cultivated by man. Of all the many varieties of this fruit, which is really a flower turned inside out with its petals and pistils contained within a fleshy hollow bowl, those from ancient Smyrna are the best. In the eighteen-eighties, a San Francisco newspaper, hoping to establish a new industry in California, imported

fig cuttings from this Turkish province and gave them to subscribers. The trees grew well, but the fruit never matured. It dried and fell to the ground.

In order to discover the reason, George Roeding was sent to Turkey by the United States Department of Agriculture. While in the fig orchards of Smyrna, he saw natives hanging branches of wild figs on trees of the cultivated variety. Curious, Roeding asked the reason and was told that the boughs kept evil spirits away; otherwise the crop would fail. The American realized that there must be an unknown scientific reason for the custom. His task was to find the connection between the inedible caprifigs borne by the wild trees and the delicious fruit of domesticated ones.

Roeding's investigation disclosed that, instead of keeping evil spirits away, the natives were making it easier for *Blastophaga psenses,* a wasp no bigger than a match head, to pollinate their fig trees. These wasps hatch out in galls—swellings in plant tissue caused by irritations—in the flowers of wild figs. The wingless and partially blind males emerge from the pupal state first, crawl to galls containing females, bite a hole and fertilize the females within. While struggling out of the galls, the winged females become covered with pollen before they fly away.

Landing on the female flowers of Smyrna figs, they enter the ovaries, seeking a place to lay their eggs. Unable to find one, they eventually settle in the blossom of a wild fig. Meanwhile, they have pollinated the Smyrna blooms with pollen from the male caprifig flowers—a process known as caprification.

Because the Turkish government was afraid of losing the American market if the secret of caprification were known—although they had no idea that it was due to wasps—it was extremely difficult to gather this information. However, by bribery, assuming a disguise and using a false name, Roeding proved an excellent detective and solved the mystery. He also managed to ship several hundred caprifigs wrapped in tin foil to the United States. Like thousands of other immigrants, the wasps they contained proved excellent workers and, through their efforts, the fig industry in California was firmly established.

MASONS

The dictionary defines dauber as an "unskilled workman," but the mud daubers, scientifically known as *Sceliphron cementarium,* are excellent masons. These wasps make cement by mixing mud with saliva and mold tubelike nests using their jaws as trowels.

Each mouthful of mud—and it takes a great many—is smoothed into a thin band encircling half the tube, being plastered into position first on one side, then on the other, forming a herringbone pattern. By erecting mud partitions, the tube is divided into six to twenty nurseries, each about an inch long. The female places paralyzed spiders and an egg in each chamber. In the spring, young adult wasps bite an opening and emerge.

Cementarium covers her masonry with an unsightly gob of cement which becomes hard as adobe. Her "daubing" may be multicolored if she has gathered mud from different sources, ranging from pale gray to black. Ofter the final plastering is studded with tiny pellets of mud, which have no value but are purely ornamental.

Other daubers' nests look like candy bars, sponges or a link of sausage. Those of *Trypoxylon fabricator* are the source of this species' common name, pipe-organ wasp. One tropical wasp not only builds its nest of mud but constructs the comb from the same material.

Abandoned daubers' nests are used by several varieties of small wasps, which divide the large cells by partitions. *Trypoxylon clavatum* often does this; the male acting as a sidewalk superintendent while his wife does all the work. Blue-mud-wasp females (*Chalybion caeruleum*) are burglars; they break into *cementarium's* house, regurgitating water over the walls to soften them. When an opening is made, the housebreakers throw out the contents of the cells, restock them, then replaster the nest in a careless manner.

While many species of potter wasps merely plaster an irregular mass of mud around a twig, or combine moss and leaves with their cement, several fashion beautifully shaped, tiny clay jugs which they fasten to vegetation.

To do this, *Eumnes fraternus* has to be a hod carrier, bricklayer and potter. Gathering clay, the female trowels a tiny saucer; then, like a human laying up a well, raises her work by going around and around. Slowly, the delicate urn takes form, bulging slightly and evenly outward. Occasionally, the potter stops and runs her antennae over her work to make sure the inside is perfectly smooth and that the outside measurements are correct. Smoothing out rough spots, she covers the entire surface with saliva and begins to draw the walls inward, finishing the jug with a neck and lip. When completed, it resembles a small-based vase, curving gently into a graceful bulge and then drawing in at the top. Finally, more saliva is applied, which makes the jug so waterproof that it can be soaked for weeks without leaking.

Paralyzed spiders are placed in the jug and the potter half closes it with a clay stopper. She then spins a fine silk thread. Firmly fastening one end to the incompleted lid, she glues an egg to the other, dropping it into the jug. It hangs like a pendulum above the caterpillars which, while unable to bite or crawl, could crush it with a muscular spasm.

When the egg shell opens it does not shatter but unrolls, adding just enough length to the thread for the larva to reach its food supply, take a quick nibble and scramble back to safety. Soon the grub is strong enough to withstand any movement made by the caterpillars and it drops off the thread, consumes all the fresh meat stocked in the urn and sleeps away the winter as a pupa.

MINERS

Like sand hogs, wasps excavate tunnels in many different types of soil. Their burrows, dug either with jaws or feet, vary in length depending upon the species. Some are only about an inch long, others extend nearly two feet below the surface. Whether they plunge vertically or curve slowly, all the burrows end in a chamber. Miners that lay more than one egg at a time place each in its own room, digging several short passages branching off from the main shaft. Here their babies

pupate all winter and emerge as adults the following summer.

No matter how they dig or the type of tunnel they excavate, fossores always scatter the soil they bring to the surface to try to hide their work. When the nest is complete, they plug the entrance hole and fly high in ever widening circles, memorizing its location by landmarks. While humans who have watched a digger wasp at work often find it impossible to find the nest after it has been closed, the wasps have no difficulty after making their orientation flight, although they become confused if a nearby object is moved.

The memory of these insects is amazing. *Bicyrtes quadrifasciata* learns the location of her nest so well that she can return high in the air, hover ten feet above the ground, drop like a helicopter and land on top of it!

Once a female has memorized the location of her nest, she goes hunting. Most fossores practice mass provisioning, stocking their chambers with paralyzed insects or spiders. Each species lays its eggs on a particular portion of the prey's body. Unlike most miners, females of some branches of the Bemecidae family engage in progressive feeding and are semisocial in habit, but each female attends to her own young.

Every time a digger returns with baby food, she opens the nest, runs in headfirst to inspect the interior, turns around in the chamber, scrambles up, seizes her prey by the head and drags it backward down the tunnel. After it is stored, she goes to the surface and reblocks the entrance hole. So deeply rooted is this procedure that Henri Fabre once made a wasp *(Sphecius speciosus)* that hunts cicadas come completely out of its burrow forty times by turning her game around so that its head faced away from the nest. Other naturalists, doing the same experiment, have frequently encountered wasps that quickly adapt themselves to this situation and pull their prey inside head last holding onto the rear end.

Miners close their burrows permanently when they have gathered enough food and laid their eggs. Some then cover the entrance with grass, others smooth dirt about to hide the depression, still others roll small stones over it. But *Ammophila* does a most remarkable thing. She picks up a pebble slightly smaller than her head, holds it firmly in her mandibles and uses it as a maul to tamp the soil down hard— one of the very few instances in which an animal, other than man, uses a tool.

PAPERMAKERS

Papermaking is an ancient art. Long before man mastered the process, wasps were chewing wood into pulp and moistening and cementing it with saliva to manufacture paper. While humans have to use special coatings for waterproofing, yellow jackets, hornets and *Polistes* do not. Nor do they need elaborate machinery to make paper of various textures. With their sharp-toothed jaws they rasp wood— hornets prefer the bark of shrubs—and collect a ball of wood fiber, then chew it until it is soft and pulpy. Because papermakers usually get their building material from weathered wood, their nests are apt to be brown, grey or yellow. However, they may gather painted wood from various sources. When they do this, their houses are striped with as many gay colors as the frosting on a birthday cupcake.

Unlike hornets and yellow jackets, which always enclose their nests with a protective covering or envelope, *Polistes* rely on the sheltered location of their homes to keep them dry. This is why this species is so particular about a nesting site—in the open, enough rain water would seep into the downward-pointing cells to drown their babies.

No wasps build more complicated nests than hornets and yellow jackets. To us, their houses are upside down. The insects start with the attic and then add lower floors as they are needed. Their nests, like those of all papermakers, are started by a queen who builds a few cells. She covers her work with side walls, gathered at the bottom with only a small hole left open for an entrance. By the time her daughters are ready to take over the task of enlarging it, the nest is as big as a golf ball.

53

The workers enlarge the attic by adding more cells made of wood pulp but soon reach the outside walls. While instinct tells them that their horizontal comb should be about six inches long, they also "know" that, if they rip the envelope to make it bigger, eggs and larvae may become chilled and not develop. They solve this problem by using two working crews. One group of wasps cuts away the walls from the inside and expands the comb, while another extends the envelope from the outside.

An envelope is really a series of skirts separated by an airspace, a system of insulation which is as effective as the use of fiber glass between the walls of human homes. To construct the outer covering, workers manufacture paper with their jaws, then press the sodden mass in place with their forelegs until it sticks. Walking backward, constantly testing their work with their antennae to see if it is thick enough, they smear the paper into long, thin strips. Each strip is patted down until it is smooth and carefully plastered so that it overlaps the one above.

When the attic is filled with eggs and larvae, another comb is suspended below it by vertical pillars. This is also attached to the envelope, but only on the upper side—an arrangement which makes the constant enlargement of the nest from the inside possible. As the community grows, more floors are added to this topsy-turvy apartment house in the same way.

The small underground nest first built in a hole by a yellow-jacket queen is also made bigger by workers. They expand the cavity, moistening the ground with regurgitated water and then rolling the softened soil into pellets which they carry away. The paper made by subterranean dwellers is much coarser than that of other species, and their nests, which bypass rocks and roots, are less strongly constructed, but are stiffened by many supports attached to the cavity walls.

In order to save time, some wise wasps have been known to chew the cardboard tags, used to identify plants, into pulp. But no matter how rushed papermakers may be, they construct new cells only on the

margin of the comb. Above the new additions are recently built cells containing eggs, topped by those holding just hatched larvae. The next section consists of fully grown larvae, while the chambers above are occupied by capped pupae. Then comes a row of empty cells from which adults have emerged, and another row of eggs. This order, which insures an even distribution of weight in the comb, is repeated over and over again.

Besides tearing down and expanding the outside walls, adding tiers of comb and making passageways between them, workers remodel the nurseries when young wasps vacate them. They bite off the jagged edges of the cells and add a smooth coating of paper in preparation for the next tenant. However, no cell is used more than three times. This explains the tremendous size of papermakers' nests—for as many as 25,000 wasps may be born in one of them in a single summer.

PARASITES

There are many wasp parasites, but, instead of accusing them of wanting "something for nothing," we should be most grateful to them.

55

Thanks to their habits, millions of harmful insects are destroyed and the balance of nature maintained.

Most of the thousands of species that practice parasitism follow the same routine. The female seeks a certain prey, pierces it with her ovipositor and lays an egg within it. The larva hatches, feeds on its host —which lives for some time—emerges, spins a cocoon and pupates, reaching adulthood in a short time.

This brief life cycle means that several generations are born annually. Therefore, it is theoretically possible for the offspring of a Braconid wasp, which lays more than one egg in a host, to consume 1,677,000,000,000 crop-destroying insects in a summer! Braconids are small—as are all parasitic wasps—but are giants compared with a Mymarmid wasp, which is only 1/120 of an inch long. These wasps and other pygmy species lay their eggs in the eggs of their host insect rather than in the adults, larvae or pupae, as do their bigger relatives.

The most remarkable eggs of any wasp parasite are those of certain members of the Chalcid family. Each one hatches out a great number of individuals, all of the same sex. In order to find damsel-fly eggs, which serve her as hosts, one Chalcid enters the water and swims beneath the surface with her wings like a penguin!

Trigonalids make sure their eggs reach a grasshopper's stomach— they hatch only when acted upon by digestive juices—by laying them on plants eaten by these pests. Some Scelionid female wasps attach themselves to the bodies of grasshoppers, matids and moths; then shed their wings. If they have chosen a host of like sex, they oviposit their eggs in those of their mount. Because of the damage they do to matids, which also destroy huge numbers of injurious insects, Scelionids are both friends and foes of man.

Members of the Cynipidae family lay their eggs in plant tissues. When they hatch (often months later) the secretions of the larvae cause a gall. Each species makes its own variety of gall, easily recognized by shape. Some gall-makers are serious parasites on fruit trees, forage crops and grains. However, galls formed on oak trees have long been used by man in the manufacture of tannic acid and ink.

Because two species of social wasps have no worker caste, they engage in parasitism. The fertilized females sneak into an unguarded community, lay their eggs and flee, leaving their babies to be reared by strangers. When they develop, the adults fly away and raise their own families in the same way. The beautiful cuckoo wasp, like the bird for which it is named, also lays its eggs in nests built by others. Another wasp that takes advantage of its relatives is the velvet ant, whose shape and fur coat account for its name. They are parasites on fossores. In the south, these colorful insects are called "cow killers" because their severe sting—extremely painful to humans—causes cattle to stampede.

The most fascinating thing about parasitism is that certain parasites are preyed upon by other parasites, which in turn serve as hosts for still smaller species; just like those wooden Billikens nestled one within the other!

8. Watching Wasps

The safest way to examine wasps' paper apartments is after they have been deserted. However, with the aid of a friendly beekeeper who is wearing sting-proof clothing, social wasps can be observed in a box covered with a fine wire mesh, with a small door cut in one end. After pulling a nest down (none should be destroyed until mid-September when wasps have but a few weeks to live), the beekeeper should place comb and the workers on it in the box. By this arrangement you can see eggs hatch, larvae spin cocoons, and adults break out of their silk

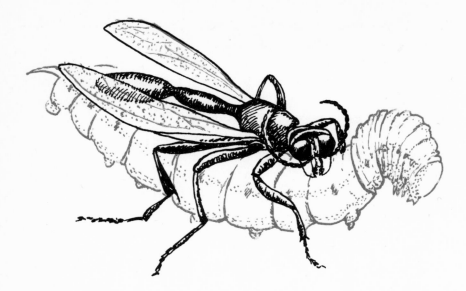

kimonos. All that has to be done is to feed the workers gobs of honey and bits of meat through the door while wearing thick gloves.

If there are no adults on the comb, try this experiment: touch the edges of the larvae's mouth with a toothpick and they will secrete saliva. The liquid will also flow if you whistle loudly. To the grubs, it sounds like vibrating wings.

By filling dishes of the same color with salted and sugared water, you can see how quickly wasps learn which is the sweet solution. You can also determine how well they "know their colors" by providing food in a colored dish. After the insects become familiar with the container, change it for one of another hue and watch the wasps learn the difference.

Solitaries offer many opportunities for field observation. You can time them as they dig their burrows in different types of soil, measure the length of their excavations, and record how long after the nest is

THREAD-WAISTED WASP

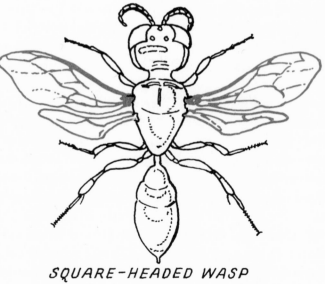

SQUARE-HEADED WASP

sealed that the young adult emerges. Vegetable coloring (used to color cakes) poured into puddles where daubers get their mud will result in red, blue or green masonry.

Any solitary wasp's cocoon will hatch in a small box padded with cotton, provided it is kept in a cool place. The box should be covered with fine wire so that the wasp can be taken outside and released when developed. Often species that nest in cavities will build their nests in a glass tube left near a popular nesting site. These too can be brought indoors and will allow all the steps of metamorphosis to be clearly seen.

Remember to keep notes of everything observed. Not only will they provide a permanent record of what you have seen, but they will also be of value to other students interested in the witchery of wasps.

9. It's Possible!

While patient observation of wasps will bring you much pleasure, there's a chance you'll discover a new fact about them. These phrases appear under hundreds of species listed in the catalogue of American wasps: "little is known" and "more observation needed." You don't have to be a scientist. Out of a hobby of watching wasps, Phil Rau, a Missouri storekeeper, added much to our knowledge of their ways.

Even if you do not add to man's information, watching wasps will make your explorations into the wonderful world of Nature more enjoyable. Always remember that, while insects can be studied in books and museums, the greatest pleasure and profit comes from watching them personally in the field.

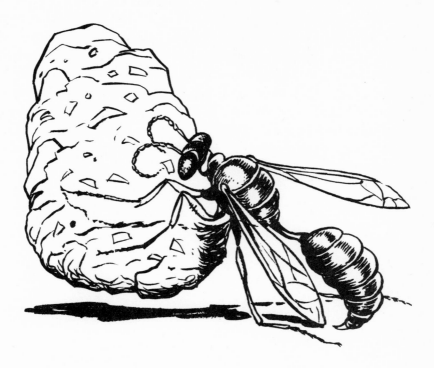

Index

S I G M U N D A . L A V I N E just missed being cradled in a theatrical trunk. His parents were permanent members of John Craig's famous stock company, and his arrival made it unnecessary for the stage manager to provide a doll whenever the play called for a baby!

Highly active while in college, he wrote features for the Boston *Sunday Post*, covered Boston University sports for two wire services, occasionally sold two-line jokes to *College Humor*, played leads in Shakespeare productions and stage-managed five annual presentations of the Gilbert and Sullivan Association. "This last experience," Sigmund Lavine maintains, "was the beginning of a search for anything by or about Gilbert and Sullivan — with the result that the bookcases in my Milton, Massachusetts, home contain books behind books dealing with the Kings of Topsy-turvydom."

After receiving his M.A., he taught in a United States Government Indian School at Belcourt, North Dakota, for two years, learned to speak both the Sioux and Cree languages and talk in sign language, had long conversations with old-timers who could remember the creak of the axles of covered wagons, and was invited to tribal dances, ceremonies and Indian Court in reservations throughout Canada and the Northwest.

Sigmund Lavine has taught in the Boston Schools for over twenty years and is now an assistant principal. He also lectures and writes literary criticism.

With his wife, their son, Jerrold, Carrie, their whippet, and Andrea ben Ghazi, their prize-winning Afghan hound, he lives in a house filled with books, fish tanks and historical china. His family enjoys cruises to South America, cross-country motor trips and truck gardening on a piece of New Hampshire land which, the author says, "contains all the rocks the glacier had and didn't know what to do with — however, we always have a pumpkin for a jack-o'-lantern."